# CONTENTS

# WELCOME SPEECHES
## for Special Days

### Cheryl Kirk-Duggan

# WELCOME SPEECHES FOR SPECIAL DAYS

**ISBN 0-687-022746**

MANUFACTURED IN THE UNITED STATES OF AMERICA

# INTRODUCTION

Religious occasions in African American churches are eminently important celebrations that are accomplished with beauty and purpose. This volume is a tool to enhance church programming and to reflect elegant, faith-seeking, life-affirming, and freedom-longing services. Most of the statements and responses provide spaces to insert the name of the church, related dates or numbers, and/or geographical places. These statements and prayers can be tailored for your own church ceremony by including the names of honorees, the community, or of helpful members where appropriate. Scripture passages are taken from the New Revised Standard Version of the Bible. Use the Occasions, Welcomes, Recitations, and Prayers to the benefit of your church and the glory of God!

# CHILDREN'S DAY

## Occasion

Jesus said: "Let the little children come to me, and do not stop them; for it is to such as these that the kingdom [the rule] of heaven belongs" (Matt. 19.14; Luke 18.15-16; Mark 10.14). Jesus blesses children. He teaches that we all come to God's kingdom as children. This means that we simply need to depend on and trust in God. Today we celebrate Jesus and rejoice that he blesses us. Children are gifts. Today we challenge the *[church name]* to love, support, teach, and mentor our children.

## Welcome

O magnify the Lord! With the joy and innocence of children, we welcome each of you to this wonderful celebration of Christian life. To the pastor, officers, members, and friends of *[church name]*, we bring you greetings! The children's department is excited about our God-given gifts and opportunities. We consider it an honor to be in charge of the services and we welcome and invite each of you to join in and participate with us. Make yourselves comfortable in the Lord.

We offer our praises, songs, prayers, and readings as a joyful noise unto the Lord. Help us celebrate! Clap your hands, tap your feet if the Lord moves you in that way. We welcome you with open hands and hearts, to experience God in this holy sanctuary. Each of us is God's child; for God created all of us. As we are made in God's image, we are to bear witness to the world. So being that witness, today we invite you to praise God and be so inspired that this joy brings you closer to God and to knowing yourself. Welcome!

## *Response*

In the name of Jesus Christ, thank you dear children and all those who work with the children's department of *[church name].* You are beautiful, gifted, and special, and we thank God for you. It is wonderful to see you and to witness all that God is doing in your lives. Allow the Lord to continue to use you and always serve Christ, for only what we do for Christ will last. We accept your welcome in the spirit of the God we serve, and look forward to this anointed service. Your words of welcome, given in the innocence and purity of children, have been a refreshing balm to our hearts.

# Recitations for Children

### 1

How blessed are we
To have and to hold,
Children to see,
Beauty to behold!

Christ gives us the task
To help and to love
As done in the past,
Spirit gifts from above.

Children are precious,
Cherished, and unique.
Their light shines among us
Their souls God to keep.

2

In all ways our children,
By God's image formed,
Are given the truth
Through His Holy Word.

Our kindness, our needs,
Our beauty, our grace
Come from Jesus' peace,
From the Savior's face.

So we just thank Christ
For giving this gift,
Kids strong and bright,
High praises we lift!

3
Spreading the gospel
Kids willingly do,
By singing and praising
God before you.

We learn and we grow
In God's tender care,
Knowing in heaven
We will meet Him there.

Until then we serve Him
Throughout this whole life.
We love the Lord Jesus
And follow His might.

## Suggested Scripture

Lord, you have been our dwelling place in all generations. Before the mountains were brought forth, or ever you had formed the earth and the world, from everlasting to everlasting, you are God. (Ps. 90.1-2)

The wolf shall live with the lamb, the leopard shall lie down with the kid, the calf and the lion and the fatling together, and a little child shall lead them. (Isa. 11.6)

"And my spirit rejoices in God my Savior." (Luke 1.47)

So we can say with confidence, "The Lord is my helper; I will not be afraid. What can anyone do to me?" (Heb. 13.6)

# GRADUATION PROGRAM DAY

## *Occasion*

Recognition is honorable and helps us to highlight the milestones in our lives. Many steps make up the ladder of achievement. That process involves work and much effort by the clergy, staff, and the supportive members of *[church name]*. Knowledge gained and lessons learned are tools that help us to be more loving, more Christlike. Education is an act of grace: a gift of God's lovingkindness that can give us insight and joyfulness. This occasion honors the successful. Every time we study God's Word and exercise our understanding in our daily lives we are a success.

## *Welcome*

The psalmist cries out words of gladness in praise of Zion in Psalm 122. In this Scripture, a group of pilgrims arrives in Jerusalem and rejoices at the unity the buildings symbolize. We honor and greet all of you whose pilgrimage has allowed you to bless us with your presence. We rejoice that the Lord has brought us together in unity to celebrate *[graduation or promotion]* day. We receive you in gladness and cordiality with open hearts. The pastor, leaders, officers, members, and friends of *[church name]* invite you to participate with us as we honor the *[graduates or students promoted]* this year.

We *[graduates/students]* represent the beautiful, the good, and the true in our lives. We are beautiful for we are God's children. We are good in that God made us that way in the beginning and we are called to do good things. We are also good in that God has given us minds to think and comprehend. One way we know truth is through Christ Jesus. We know truth and beauty as we use all our God-given gifts to help us actively love and make a difference. We welcome you here! We welcome you to explore the good, true, and beautiful within because Christ is here in us and with us. Welcome!

## Response

Thank you, graduates, for such a wonderful welcome. This is indeed a special time in the life of [church name]. What a sweet Spirit in the house of the Lord, when the people of God can gather together in celebration of achievement. It has been only the grace of God that has brought us thus far. All of the graduates deserve to be honored in this special way, for graduation is a holy ceremony. It is the time we publicly give honor to God for helping us to succeed. So, your welcome is accepted in Christian love. God bless you!

# A Graduation Recitation Speech

Certificates and diplomas
Announce to the world
The hard work and dedication of
Families and friends,
Students and educators
To better ourselves
And the rest of humanity
For the glory of God.

Ideas, concepts, thoughts,
Visions, drawings, experiments,
Speeches, poems, essays,
Athletic events, a collegiate bowl,
Express part of us,
Express part of God,
In whose image we are made.

Let's honor education,
Let's work passionately,
Let's do well.
God's grace bestows our gifts,
Behooves us to excel,
To feel good about ourselves,
And never stop learning,
Never stop caring,
Never stop dreaming.

## Suggested Scripture

[Lord, we are] your servant[s]; give [us] understanding, so that [we] may know your decrees. (Ps. 119:125)

They do not know, nor do they comprehend; for their eyes are shut, so that they cannot see, and their minds as well, so that they cannot understand. (Isa. 44.18)

And they came and said to him, "[Jesus], we know that you are sincere, and show deference to no one; for you do not regard people with partiality, but teach the way of God in accordance with truth." (Mark 12.14*a)*

To one is given through the Spirit the utterance of wisdom, and to another the utterance of knowledge according to the same Spirit. (1 Cor. 12.8)

# HOMECOMING DAY/
# CHURCH ANNIVERSARY

## *Occasion*

Family and community building are central to African American life. Extended family existed in Africa, during slavery, and continues today. Blood defines only some of our kinships. We have "cousins," "aunts," and "uncles" through association. We bless God for the institution of family, especially for our children and our elders who know God, speak truth, and show us how to love. With gratitude and joy, we the members of [church name] remember all of our kinfolk as we observe this homecoming/church anniversary.

## *Welcome*

"I was glad when they said to me, 'Let us go to the house of the LORD!' " (Ps. 122.1). We know gladness because we are called to praise God. Today, we, the pastors, officers, and members of [church name] are glad to welcome you to praise the Lord, be restored, and to experience renewal and recommitment. The power of love and togetherness is the foundation of this worship service. Through God's grace [church name] is here as a testament of the faith and hope of God's people. With anticipating spirits and joyful hearts, we invite you to be here with us, participate, and have a good time.

On behalf of *[church name]*, we embrace you in Christ's love. We hold true to the communal spirit of the church. We invite you to embrace that spirit at church, home, work, and play. We welcome you to the profound experience of being with the Body of Christ. Be welcome. Be well. Be a part of our family. Welcome!

## *Response*

This is the day that the Lord has made, let us rejoice and be glad in it. Thank you for that beautiful welcome. What a day! We are with family, friends, and church members, some of whom we may not have seen in a while. This is the time we get together as a church family and reflect on our history and community. Praise God for one another! God has given us to one another. What a welcome, what a special time.

## A Recitation for Homecoming/ Church Anniversary

Mama and Daddy,
Big Mama and Pa Pa,
Sister, brother, uncle, aunt, cousins and friends,
Lil' Sis, Big Bro, Junior,
Nana,
Husband, wife,
Pastor, preacher,
Deacon, trustee,
Stewardess board,
Ushers, choir directors,
Missionary society,
People we love,
All God's people,
Kin and others,
By blood, selection, ordination, and choice,
Freedom to love, to grow,
Freedom to live and forgive,
Families existing in love,
With a heritage to pass on:
Pictures, quilts, Bibles, memories,
Joys, sorrows, hopes.
How blessed we are,
For we are God's family!

## *Suggested Scripture*

Let [us] hear of your steadfast love in the morning, for in you [we] put my [our] trust. (Ps. 143.8)

"As for me and my household, we will serve the LORD." (Josh. 24.15*b)*

[Jesus] said to them, "Where is your faith?" They were afraid and amazed, and said to one another, "Who then is this, that he commands even the winds and the water, and they obey him?" (Luke 8.25)

And hope does not disappoint us, because God's love has been poured into our hearts through the Holy Spirit that has been given to us. (Rom. 5.5)

# MOTHER'S DAY

## Occasion

Today is the day we join others throughout the world as we honor the love of mothers. God is symbolized in ways we experience mothering. We are mothered and held in the Lord's bosom, where we experience nurture and care. This day we honor the women who gave us birth and non-biological mothers who daily nurture and pray for us. This is mother's day!

## Welcome

Greetings in the name of Christ Jesus! We, the members of *[church name]*, deem it a privilege to welcome each of you to our Mother's Day celebration. We lift our voices, making a joyful noise unto the Lord in thanksgiving for mothers everywhere. We cherish the courage, fortitude, and insight of mothers, evident when they have made a way out of no way.

We honor the ministry of mothers. Mothers are special. They guide and lead us. Mothers of the church are noble persons of authority and understanding. We look to them for wisdom and spiritual teaching. Mothers have offered hundreds of intercessory prayers, soothed thousands of fevers, made or selected countless Easter outfits, and baked or bought dozens of cookies for vacation Bible school.

Mothers have passed on folk wisdom, given advice, learned when to keep silent, and helped rear grandchildren. Mothers love the Lord and walk by faith. Today we thank God for all mothers and celebrate their true spirit of love, nurture, compassion, leadership, patience, creativity, and joy. Welcome to our church home, welcome to our hearts. Welcome to all mothers and all mothers' children. Welcome!

## *Response*

The Spirit of the living God is truly in this place! What a wonderful welcome for a most special day, the day we honor mothers! As a mother, I can truly say that it is a blessing to be in the house of the Lord on a day like today. And, I think that I speak for many of us when I say that if it had not been for the Lord on my side, O Lord, O Lord, where would I be? Thank you for that most gracious welcome. There is nothing like being welcomed in the house of the Lord. Because no matter what's going on outside, in Jesus' house, I know I am at home. Praise the Lord!

# A Recitation for Mothers

Who are mothers?
Mothers cook, clean, love, heal, and care.
Who are mothers?
Mothers are always prepared.

Who are mothers?
Mothers wipe our tears and make us smile.
Who are mothers?
No matter what the test, mothers will walk a mile.

Who are mothers?
When it comes to their babies, mothers know no fear.
Who are mothers?
Their precious loved ones, they pray for and hold dear.

Who are mothers?
Mothers teach with love and respect.
Who are mothers?
Without them, what would we have left?

Lord God, thank you for mothers!

# Suggested Scripture

For it was you who formed my inward parts; you knit me together in my mother's womb. I praise you, for I am fearfully and wonderfully made. Wonderful are your works; that I know very well. (Ps. 139.13-14)

Then justice will dwell in the wilderness, and righteousness abide in the fruitful field. The effect of righteousness will be peace, and the result of righteousness, quietness and trust forever. (Isa. 32.16-17)

When [Jesus] saw their faith, he said, "Friend, your sins are forgiven you." (Luke 5.20)

And this is my prayer, that your love may overflow more and more with knowledge and full insight to help you to determine what is best. (Phil. 1.9-10*a*)

# FATHER'S DAY

## *Occasion*

Blessings and glory to God and congratulations to all
fathers. Fathers, our male parents, come in all shapes and
forms, with many desires, dreams, avocations, and abilities. The Bible tells the stories of many fathers and their
struggles to be good parents as part of God's call on their
lives. Abraham, Isaac, Jacob, Joseph, Moses, Samuel, Saul,
and David wrestled with being a father to their immedi-
ate family and to the nation of Israel. Jesus speaks of God
as Abba, Father, to denote an intimate, deeply felt rela-
tionship of responsibility and love. Today we join people
throughout the world as we sacredly reflect on the ministry of fatherhood. Today, we celebrate the many fathers
in our lives: biological, adopted, extended family, and
mentors.

## *Welcome*

Glory and honor to God, and blessings in the name of
Christ Jesus. The pastor, officers, and members of *[church
name]* welcome you in joy as we participate in our annual
Father's Day program. We welcome you to join with us in

honoring the nobility, elegance, and demands of being a father. We welcome and invite you to recognize the fathers of the church, the African American fathers of history who have had dreams, have offered intercessory prayers, have guided us, encouraged us, loved us, taught us to be strong, to use our imagination and improve ourselves and our communities. We thank God for fathers.

We are grateful for fathers who know Jesus and realize that God's grace, full of mercy and justice, is the force that gives all of us life and the opportunity to be fathers. We welcome you to reflect on your own fathers and perhaps on your role as a father. We welcome you to be at home with us and to let us take care of you. We welcome you to visit at any time. Welcome, welcome, welcome. Welcome, this holy Father's name. In the name of God the Father, welcome!

## Response

Blessed be the name of the Lord! This is Father's Day, a holy day, and I respond in thankfulness to your welcome. On behalf of visiting friends, in extending this thanks, I pray that we may live up to the expectations of your welcome. We are so happy to see all these wonderful fathers, and are truly happy about the Almighty Father. This is a most auspicious occasion, and let us have a blessed time in the Lord!

# A Recitation for Fathers

Fathers are noble and strong,
Full of courage, full of feelings.
Fathers are gentle spirits,
Wise and giving.
Fathers are providers,
Taking care of their families.
Fathers are loving,
Spreading hope and joy with their laughter.
Fathers are reliable,
Always ready to lend a helping hand.
Fathers are understanding,
Sharing truth and knowledge to their loved ones.
Fathers are resourceful,
Knowing how best to handle problems.
Fathers are protectors,
Sheltering their children under their wings.
Fathers are teachers,
Disciplining with care and restraint
Fathers are leaders,
Showing the right path.
Fathers are real men, defenders of the faith, special gifts
  from God.

## Suggested Scripture

I will sing of your steadfast love, O LORD, forever; with my mouth I will proclaim your faithfulness to all generations. (Ps. 89.1)

Listen, children, to a father's instruction, and be attentive, that you may gain insight. (Prov. 4.1)

"No one can serve two masters; for a slave will either hate the one and love the other, or be devoted to the one and despise the other. You cannot serve God and wealth." (Matt. 6.24)

Now we have received not the spirit of the world, but the Spirit that is from God, so that we may understand the gifts bestowed on us by God. (1 Cor. 2.12)

# WOMEN'S DAY

## *Occasion*

Today we celebrate the annual Women's Day celebration of *[church name]*. Women's Day is a special event in our church's life. This day brings our church family and guests together to help us fulfill our Christian mission and outreach. The women of *[church name]* form a cloud of witnesses to the world about what Jesus has done and is doing for us. We salute the women of *[church name]* as they press on in Christ Jesus to the mark of higher calling. Through God's grace and in faith; they stand tall with other women, men, and children as united in love to do God's work.

## *Welcome*

To the pastor, other distinguished pulpit guests, officers and members of *[church name]*, sisters and brothers in Christ Jesus, an invitation to meet in God's house is always a blessed time. We have come to praise God, to celebrate our community, and to celebrate being women. We, the women of *[church name]*, stand together in the name of Christ Jesus and welcome you. We welcome you to celebrate our divine goodness in song, scripture, and the preached Word. We arise, with God's help, as women of courage, ready to do God's will, to do justice, walk humbly, and befriend our neighbors. We unite as women to serve the community and ourselves. Through Christ's loving grace, we leap over oppression from the outside and the inside. Blessed are the women who listen to what Jesus says. We welcome you! We welcome you to this Women's Day program. The doors to the church, to the Body of Christ are always open. If there is anything we can do to make you feel more loved and cared for, please let us know. We are here to serve.

## *Response*

Thank you, thank you, thank you! What a glorious welcome! We know that women serve in the church at all capacities and this is the special time we set aside to honor them. So we accept your welcome for such a lovely program. Thank you for the opportunity to worship in this holy sanctuary. Thank you for the invitation to participate in a program of praise to God Almighty. We will lift up holy hands to the wonderful God we serve. Blessed be our Lord and Savior Jesus Christ!

# A Recitation for Women

We sing the word *WOMAN!*
That is who we are:
Strong, black, beautiful, bold,
Warm, blessed, faithful.

Women are God's created.
We are made in God's image.
We are daughters of God.
We live the sacred life.

Women are special!
We are happy, sad, passive, energetic,
Imaginative, elaborate, beautiful:
We all exist in God's glory.

Women are daughters of God!
Strong and well and whole.
We live the sacred life,
Teach and learn and do ministry.

Women love themselves.
We love ourselves well.
Living, regal queens,
We are God's chosen in the world.

Praise be to God!
Praise be to God!

## Suggested Scripture

This is the day that the Lord has made; let us rejoice and be glad in it. (Ps. 118.24)

And hope does not disappoint us, because God's love has been poured into our hearts through the Holy Spirit that has been given to us. (Rom. 5.5)

"As for me, I would seek God, and to God I would commit my cause." (Job 5.8)

"Whatever you ask for in prayer with faith, you will receive." (Matt. 21.22)

# MEN'S DAY

## *Occasion*

To the pastor, officers, pulpit dignitaries, members, and visitors of *[church name]*, it is celebration time in the life of our church. Today is Men's Day. We come in the name of Jesus, empowered by the Holy Spirit, to lift up the Christian life and to offer thanksgiving for the opportunity to be Christian fathers, husbands, brothers, and friends. We celebrate being created in God's image. We celebrate being men. We celebrate our partnership with all men and women, especially with those who claim an allegiance to God as revealed in Christ Jesus. We stand victorious for the Lord; our songs lift up to Zion; our prayers tell of God's goodness and mercy to us. We salute the men of *[church name]* as we grow in love, gentleness, strength, courage, and grace. We join with our faith community to do all that we do in God's glory.

## *Welcome*

To the pastor, officers, members, and friends of *[church name]:* It is good, so good to gather together to glorify God! The Lord has blessed the men of this church to love and serve the Lord and the Body of Christ. We welcome you to our Christ-filled home; we welcome you as a member of the family of God, to join us in praise and prayer. How good it is to come together! We, the men of *[church name]*, welcome you in the name of Jesus. We delight in sharing our skills and gifts in this service and in our lives like other African men who have gone before: church leader, St. Augustine of Hippo of North Africa; educator and Masonic founder, Prince Hall; and scientist and inventor, Benjamin Banneker. We welcome you to join us to serve the Lord and commit our lives to the good of the church, our community, our people. We welcome you here. Know that you have a home with us. The doors of this church are always open to you. Welcome!

## *Response*

What an honor to be welcomed by you today! We are happy and pleased to join with you in this celebration of men. From all the powerful men of history, to the blessed men that serve the church today, we stand on the shoulders of powerful role models. These great models of men inspire us to become workers for the Lord. Thank you for the chance to share in a worship service of praise to God. It is God who lifts us up everyday; it is God who is our strength; it is God who is our help. As men of God we shout glory hallelujah for all He has done, is doing, and will do in our lives! Amen!

## Recitation For Men

Men stand with the Lord,
The foundation of the Creator and Maker of all.
We are strong and weak, rich and poor.
Do not define us by what we do and who we know;
We belong to God.

Men worship the Lord and care for family.
We plant and build and play.
We are strong, we care.
Do not define us by what you see as a mask;
We feel and we love deeply.

Men are proud of our fathers, and respect our mothers.
Our sisters and brothers are closer than many.
Our friends share our pains, our mates share our bonds.
Do not define us by what society says,
We are bold and gentle and free.

Men remember our history, our fight for freedom.
We know that we are proud, black, and beautiful.
We organize, because we are somebody.
Do not define us by the limitations of time.
God holds us up in power for all the world to behold!

## *Suggested Scripture*

Happy are those who make the LORD their trust, who do not turn to the proud, to those who go astray after false gods. (Ps. 40.4)

For you shall worship no other god, because the Lord, whose name is Jealous, is a jealous God. (Exod. 34.14)

"This is my commandment, that you love one another as I have loved you. No one has greater love than this, to lay down ones' life for one's friends." (John 15.12-13)

My brothers and sisters, whenever you face trials of any kind, consider it nothing but joy, because you know that the testing of your faith produces endurance; and let endurance have its full effect, so that you may be mature and complete, lacking in nothing. (James 1.2-4)

# PASTOR ANNIVERSARY/ APPRECIATION DAY

## *Occasion*

From the times of Abraham to Esther, Jesus and Paul, Phoebe and Priscilla, from Sojourner Truth and Frederick Douglass to our own *[name of pastor and name of spouse, if married]*, men and women have accepted God's call on their lives to serve, nurture, and guide faithful believers. These persons study, teach, and preach God's Word, visit the sick and troubled, marry the beloved, baptize those new in the faith, consecrate and serve the Lord's Supper of Eucharist, counsel the concerned, bury the dead, work for justice and freedom for the oppressed, head building projects, press for outreach and discipleship, and serve as CEO with Christ as the Head with the support of the congregation. Today we honor our pastor. Today we honor *[name of pastor and name of spouse, if married]*, for serving God here at *[church name]*. As we celebrate today, let us embrace a hopeful imagination and a loving spirit that we, as pastor and church, may live and teach the good news of Christ Jesus.

# Welcome

To the pastor *[and spouse]*, officers, members of *[church name]*, visitors, and friends, we greet you in our Lord's most precious name on the occasion of our pastor's appreciation. Today we honor our pastor *[and spouse]*. We celebrate the gifts and the impact our pastor is giving to this body and the larger community. We stand before God and you with grateful hearts and hopeful anticipation that everyone will here receive blessings and inspiration in this service.

Our leaders are our guides. They inspire us to be open to God's will in our lives, for we all have a ministry. God created each of us and has anointed each of us with unique talents and special ways of participating in God's world. Each of us, as members of the church, are to minister in our daily lives to our families, friends, and neighbors. We welcome you today to celebrate God's call on all our lives as we remember *[name of pastor and spouse]* with special prayers, offerings, and love. We invite each of you to rejoice in the Lord, give thanks and praise in all we say and do! We welcome you to join us in praising God, honoring our pastor, and celebrating this office of ministry. Welcome!

## A Prayer for the Pastor

Glorious Redeemer, our Lord Jesus Christ, we praise Your name, Your everlasting grace. Your bounty is marvelous, Your love for creation is untiring. It is this love that sustains us and has given us the vision of the church and church leadership. We celebrate, O God, your gift of pastoral service to the church. We thank you for pastors and chaplains who serve in churches, hospitals, and other institutions throughout the world.

We ask special grace for our pastor and his/her family, their lives and ministry. Give them serenity and joy in their walk, wisdom and knowledge in their goals, and clarity and discernment in their life's challenges. O Lord, as a church, help us to be Christlike to our pastor, church staff, and to one another. Help us to work together to bring your Word to those who are dying of spiritual malnutrition. Gracious Creator, be the rock, shield, comforter, and teacher for Pastor [_____]. Give our pastor a sense of humor and the strength to stand against powers and principalities, to preach in season and out of season, to have the courage to use fully Your holy gifts. Help us to love and appreciate our pastor. We honor and praise Your holiness and grace for sending this shepherd to lead us, and may we do Your will, O God, in serving You. Amen.

## Suggested Scripture

Set a guard over my mouth, O LORD; keep watch over the door of my lips.
(Ps. 141.3)

"I [the Lord] will give you shepherds [pastors] after my own heart, who will feed you with knowledge and understanding." (Jer. 3.15)

"And teaching them to obey everything that I [Jesus] have commanded you. And remember, I am with you always, to the end of the age." (Matt. 28.20)

If you put these instructions before the brothers and sisters, you will be a good servant of Christ Jesus, nourished on words of the faith and of the sound teaching that you have followed. (1 Tim. 4.6)

# YOUTH DAY

## *Occasion*

Paul exhorts us, "Let no one despise your youth, but set the believers an example in speech and conduct, in love, in faith, in purity" (1 Timothy 4.12). We, as the youth of *[church name]*, stand before you as young men and women blessed and ordained of God. As young people, we are called together in love, to grow collectively and individually, to fulfill God's vision of peace for them on earth. By honoring our youth, we express our joy at the beauty, strength, and potential of God's precious creation. Thanks be to God for our young people, because in them God is expressing the hopes and dreams of the community. Today is the day we look to our youth as shining stars in our church community today, not just tomorrow. Today is a special day. Today is Youth Day! Praise the Lord!

## *Welcome*

We welcome you with open, happy hearts and gratitude as we celebrate our Youth Day at *[church name]*. On behalf of our pastor, officers, and members, we welcome you to join with the singing, praising, and sharing of our youth. Let us all lift up our voices to the Lord. Youth can praise the Lord too! We are here to lift up the name of God. We are growing in the Lord. We are thankful for parents, pastor, church family, and community that encourage us in the faith. Without the leadership and support of others, we would not be here. So sit back, relax, and glorify God in this holy house. Thank you for coming to our service. You are at home. Feel free to worship as the Holy Spirit leads, for this is the day that the Lord has made. Let us rejoice and be glad in it! Welcome!

## A Prayer for Youth

Dear Lord God Almighty, in the blessed name of Jesus, we lift up the youth of *[church name].* They are beautiful, anointed, intelligent, and talented gifts made in Your image, and precious in Your sight. Jesus, please hold them and keep them in Your tender care. Help them through all the difficulties of life and all the forces that come against them. Only by Your might can they survive the tempests and storms that living in this world can bring. You know the various trials and temptations that face them at every turn. You know the ups and the downs.

Place your tender arms of mercy around them and protect them from all manner of evil and oppression. Bless them by the power of Your Holy Spirit, and fill them with Your love, and they will give You the honor and glory and praise. In Christ Jesus' name, Amen.

## Suggested Scriptures

O my God, in you [we] trust; do not let [us] be put to shame; do not let [our] enemies exult over [us]. (Ps. 25.2)

From new moon to new moon, and from sabbath to sabbath, all flesh shall come to worship before me, says the LORD. (Isa. 66.23)

"But I say to you that listen, love your enemies, do good to those who hate you." (Luke 6.27)

For I am longing to see you so that I may share with you some spiritual gift to strengthen you—or rather so that we may be mutually encouraged by each other's faith, both yours and mine. (Rom. 1.11-12)

# CHOIR ANNIVERSARY DAY

## *Occasion*

In Judges 5, Deborah and Barak sang as they led Israel and blessed the Lord. Singing is an act of praise in which individuals and congregations make music in joyful noise to the Lord. Church choirs are groups of people that make music in adoration, praise, and glory of God. Choirs are an integral part of the worship service and the life of the church. Today we rejoice and celebrate the gifts and contributions of the *[name of the choir].* Today we offer three challenges: first, we thank the choir and challenge them to continue to grow in God's grace. Second, we challenge those musically gifted who have not yet become a part of *[church name]* choirs to participate. God gave us talents. We multiply our talents a hundred-fold when we sing. Those who sing once, pray twice. Third, we challenge the congregation to sing with praise for the spiritual well-being, anointing, and ministry of *[name of choir].*

As we honor this angelic chorus, we pray for their continual renewal. We pray that God anoints *[names of musicians]* as they direct, accompany, teach, inspire, and serve. May each note they sing radiate with Spirit-filled power from on high.

# Welcome

Make a joyful noise unto the Lord, all you lands, all you people everywhere! With voices, instruments, and song, we welcome each of you to this annual choir anniversary celebration.

To the pastor, officers, members, and friends of *[church name]*, greetings and joy! The *[choir name]* members are blessed by your presence and are grateful for the opportunity to lift up the Lord's name in song. Serving you today is our ministry. Feel free to join in with a hand clap, a nod of the head, or a great Amen!

We come before you in awe of God and of the many talents and musical gifts bestowed upon us. We rejoice that you are here to share in this service of the Word and song. Just as God created birds of song to serenade the divinely created handiwork we call the world, God has given us many songs to sing, and many blessings to sing about.

## Prayer for the Choir

O great Creator of sound and Conductor of heavenly symphonies! O Ancient of Days, how magnificent and eloquent you are! Every song, every musical work—combination of sound and silence, of melody and rhythm—every created utterance is yours.

Gracious Lord, we thank you for the beauty and majesty of all song and for those who have sung praises to your most holy name. Blessed Director of all life, fix our hearts, minds, bodies, and spirits that we might always sing for your glory. Help us to be joyful, willing vessels that carry healing, inspiring sound. Let the meditations of our hearts, and the proclamations of our lives in Christ Jesus be acceptable in your sight. Amen.

## Suggested Scriptures

O [our] strength, [we] will sing praises to you, for you, O God, are [our] fortress, the God who shows [us] steadfast love. (Ps. 59.17)

Sing and rejoice, O daughter Zion! For lo, I will come and dwell in your midst, says the LORD. (Zech. 2.10)

As [Jesus] was now approaching the path down from the Mount of Olives, the whole multitude of the disciples began to praise God joyfully with a loud voice for all the deeds of power that they had seen. (Luke 19.37)

About midnight Paul and Silas were praying and singing hymns to God, and the prisoners were listening to them. Suddenly there was an earthquake, so violent that the foundations of the prison were shaken; and immediately all the doors were opened and everyone's chains were unfastened. (Acts 16.25-26)

# AFRICAN AMERICAN HISTORY CELEBRATION

## *Occasion*

Carter G. Woodson, the founder of Black History celebrations, knew the importance of knowing one's self and history. Today we celebrate Black History. Let us extend this occasion to a daily celebration of who we are and whose we are. We are noble, elegant creatures of God. We have a past, a present, and a future in Christ Jesus. Millions have gone before us. Many have taught, produced, shared, and cared. We honor the persons and recall the events of African American History. We recognize the historical heritage of *[church name]* and *[city]*. We pray that God will help us to learn about and learn from the past, to better live with self-esteem and self-awareness today, to better prepare for the time when the future tomorrow becomes today. May there come a time when the interaction and empowerment of all society reaches a point where we all celebrate African American history daily.

# Welcome

The hymn writer says, "We've a story to tell to the nations!" We have many stories to tell about God and the Bible, about ourselves, our culture, our realities. Telling stories helps us to build community; we reflect the lives of one another and celebrate similarities and differences. Today we celebrate the sharing of stories of an African American experience.

To the pastor, officers, members, and friends of *[church name]*, greetings and blessings in Jesus' name! We celebrate the heritage of your family and our collective families. We honor the stories and traditions of the African American experience in *[name of city]*. We bless God for the history of *[church name]* and our ministry to our church family, friends, and one another. We welcome you to join us in honoring the many accomplishments and contributions of African Americans to our lives and to this country.

Welcome to our celebration! We invite you to learn more about who you are and whose you are. Again, welcome!

# A Prayer for African American History Month

O God of life and history, who acted in the beginning and acts today, we praise your eternal mercy and justice that sustains us in our strength and frailty. We thank you for the lives of slaves, who praised your name despite the tyranny that oppressed them. We thank you for those who always protested injustice and rallied for change and transformation in the home, church, and society. Help us to name the evils of the past and present. Empower us, O God, to never deny who we are, and to know just how beautiful You have made us. Help us, dear author and finisher of our faith, to have a true sense of the accomplishments of African Americans to have a vision of possibility about all we can be and do. O Redeemer, we thank you for life, health, and strength. Help us to live this day so well that when the history of this day is written, we can hear God say about today: "Well done, my good and faithful servant!"

## Suggested Scripture

No weapon that is fashioned against [us] shall prosper, and [we] shall confute every tongue that rises against [us] in judgment. This is the heritage of the servants of the Lord and their vindication from me, says the Lord. (Isa. 54.17)

Let bronze be brought from Egypt; let Ethiopia hasten to stretch its hands to God. (Ps. 68.31)

"For I was hungry and you gave me food, I was thirsty and you gave me something to drink, I was a stranger and you welcomed me, I was naked and you gave me clothing, I was sick and you took care of me, I was in prison and you visited me." (Matt. 25.35-36)

Therefore, since we are surrounded by so great a cloud of witnesses, let us also lay aside every weight and the sin that clings so closely, and let us run with perseverance the race that is set before us, looking to Jesus the pioneer and perfecter of our faith. (Heb. 12.1-2*a*)

# POETRY AND PRAYERS

## *Prayer for Strength*

O Sovereign Lord, leader of all leaders, our Shepherd and Savior: we thank you on this wonderful morning for life, health, strength, for community building, and for leadership. We thank you, O God, O Ancient of Days, for the call on our lives to be followers and leaders. Let us realize that the grace of our Lord is sufficient; that "[we] can do all things through him who strengthens [us]" (Phil. 4.13). For times do get rough, and the storms of trials blow. Give us the fortitude to hold on to Your unchanging hand. Bless us with power from on high. Anoint us with Your wisdom, grace, and love to move on through. Amen.

## *Prayer to God's Glory*

O Lord, our help in ages past, our hope for years to come: We approach Your throne with thankful hearts and abounding joy, praising your holy name. We praise You, O God, with song, prayer, and the gospel. We celebrate the call You have on our lives. We bless You for the abundant blessings, constant help, and protection over our lives. Help us to work together for the good of the church and the world. Teach us how to let go of hurt and disagreement. You have brought us a mighty long way, and we just say, hallelujah! Help us, Gentle Savior, as You daily look beyond our faults to our needs. Lord, we are open to You for Your grace of cleansing reconciliation that wipes away not only the tears of sorrow, but also the stains of greed, selfishness, false pride, jealousy, bitterness, and prejudice. We accept your visions of love and compassion as our pathway to unspeakable joy, trust, and salvation for those who still do not know You. As we continue to grow, we look toward the altar, leaving all our cares and hurts. Be our joy in all we do. Amen.

## Hand in Hand, Together

We meet, we pray, we sing, we work
In the name of Jesus,
In the power of the Holy Spirit,
To spread the gospel message,
To shout to the world,
Who we are, who we are!
We are children of Jesus!
We're striving to be Christlike,
Trying to make heaven our home on earth.

God calls us at work and at play
To love the Lord with all our heart;
To love our neighbors as ourselves!
Love is listening, love is doing, love is sharing
With others, as if with Christ.
Hand in hand, together,
Creating a better day.
Moving toward the kingdom
And the sweet by and by.

## *Walking Up the King's Highway*

Everyone has a load to bear,
As we march to Zion,
But none of us carry the Lion's share.
We must do our part
To give the message from the heart.
In a world where there is much despair
We often forget to share this hope—
That Jesus Christ does care.
So the story we tell,
As tell it we shall,
For the love of God will never end,
And on this love we can depend.

## *Prayer for Honor and the Church*

Lord, You have said, "On this rock I will build my church, and the gates of Hades will not prevail against it" (Matt. 16.18*b*). We praise You for the gifts of yourself, the grounds and places of worship, the abilities and means that enable frail human beings to participate in this process.

O Lord, You are so great and magnificent. From the beginning of time to our biblical ancestors; from the New Testament until today—You have created and given us much in love. So we thank You Lord, thank You for these gifts of unconditional love. We thank You that You are always reconciling us to You. Gracious Creator, through Your covenants with us, through the prophets, through Jesus, you continue to bring us back into relationships.

For these acts and so many more, you are worthy of praise. Lord, help us to be willing to do what you require: "to do justice, and to love kindness, and to walk humbly with [our] God" (Micah 6.8). Teach us to respect and honor You and all that is dedicated to Your glory, including ourselves. In the name of Jesus Christ, our Lord and Savior, Amen.

## Our Church House, Our Home

The steeple stands tall,
Rosebushes look grand, and windows sparkle so.
Laughing children run to and fro
In our house, a special place for all.
Dear God, You've given us a house and home,
A joyous, spiritual place to roam
Midst family and friends and saints
Who come to learn, to grow,
To share, to love, to reach.
We lift our heads and hearts
To you, great God and Friend.
We sit, sing, laugh, and pray
As we gather in Your name.
Thank You, O Mighty One.
Your house is our home.

## Christian Pledge

Lord, we pledge:

To be witnesses of the power of Christ Jesus in our lives and to encourage the well-being and spiritual growth of others.

To serve all with a spirit of love regardless of race, creed, gender, and class as Jesus served during His ministry on earth.

To support sharing the gospel by listening to and living by the preached and written Word.

To participate in the rituals and rules of the church.

To be a part of the teaching and learning witness of the church.

To tithe and to give of our time and talents as God has so blessed us.

To practice God's ministry of forgiving.

To be whom God has called us to be.

# Notes

# Notes

*Notes*

# Notes

# Notes

*Notes*